CAROLE WALTER

Cakes

Photography by SIMON WHEELER

THE MASTER CHEFS

TED SMART

CAROLE WALTER studied patisserie and the culinary arts with notable chefs in France, Austria, Italy and Denmark. She is a charter member of the International Association of Culinary Professionals and past president of the New York Association of Cooking Teachers. A teacher, writer and consultant, she has frequently appeared on American television.

She is the author of a number of books, including *Great Cakes*, which won the Best Baking Book of 1992 award from The James Beard Foundation.

Photograph by James Healy

CONTENTS

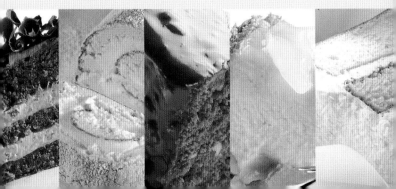

A meal without

dessert is like a play

without an ending.

INTRODUCTION

Looking at this book as a tiny treasury of treats, I have filled
it with some of my favourite recipes to satisfy sweet cravings
at any time of day or for any occasion. Sometimes I want a
cake that is chewy or has lots of crunch, sometimes I
unabashedly crave chocolate, but at times fresh fruit will be
my choice. I selected these ten recipes for their ease of
preparation and use of familiar and accessible ingredients.

Plain tea-style cakes such as Buttermilk Pound Cake are
always on my guests' 'most-wanted' list, while for celebrations
I like an impressive layer cake. I have given a choice of three:
light and delicate Snowflake Layer Cake, rich and colourful
Chocolate Raspberry Torte and a terrifically chocolaty
Fudge-nut Candy Cake.

No book of cakes would be complete without a special
cheesecake. Golden Apple Cheesecake is a refreshing
combination of cream cheese and fruit on a gingersnap crust.
When I want something sweet but light, I opt for an
almond-crusted Cinnamon Angel Cake. I hope you enjoy
making these cakes as much as I do.

Carole Walter

BUTTERMILK POUND CAKE

250 G/9 OZ PLAIN FLOUR

1 TEASPOON BAKING POWDER

½ TEASPOON BICARBONATE OF
    SODA

¼ TEASPOON GROUND MACE

¼ TEASPOON SALT

175 G/6 OZ UNSALTED BUTTER, AT
    ROOM TEMPERATURE

1 TEASPOON GRATED ORANGE ZEST

250 G/9 OZ CASTER SUGAR

3 LARGE EGGS, SEPARATED

1 TEASPOON VANILLA ESSENCE

250 ML/8 FL OZ BUTTERMILK

¼ TEASPOON CREAM OF TARTAR

ICING SUGAR, FOR DUSTING

SERVES 8–10

Preheat the oven to 180°C/350°F/
Gas Mark 4. Butter a 24 cm/
9½ inch kugelhopf tin or a 24 cm/
9½ inch round, 8 cm/3 inch deep
cake tin (a kugelhopf tin will mean
the cake cooks more evenly). Dust
the tin with flour; shake out any
excess flour.

Sift the flour, baking powder,
bicarbonate of soda, mace and salt
together three times.

Using an electric mixer on
medium speed, cream the butter

with the orange zest. Beating
continuously, gradually add 175 g/
6 oz of the sugar, taking 4–6
minutes to incorporate it. Add the
egg yolks, one at a time, beating
well after each addition, then beat
in the vanilla essence.

Fold in the flour mixture
alternately with the buttermilk,
beginning and ending with flour.

In a clean bowl, whisk the egg
whites until frothy. Add the cream
of tartar and beat until soft peaks
form. Gradually add the remaining
sugar, beating well to form a soft
meringue. Fold a quarter of the
meringue into the cake mixture,
then gently fold in the remaining
meringue. Spoon into the cake tin
and smooth the top.

Bake for 55–60 minutes or until
golden brown and coming away
from the sides of the tin. Leave the
tin on a cooling rack for about 20
minutes, then turn out the cake.
Serve dusted with icing sugar.

DOUBLE CHOCOLATE CAKE
with dates and walnuts

175 G/6 OZ DATES, COARSELY
    CHOPPED
250 ML/8 FL OZ BOILING WATER
1 TEASPOON BICARBONATE OF
    SODA
200 G/7 OZ PLAIN FLOUR
1½ TABLESPOONS UNSWEETENED
    COCOA POWDER, SIFTED
½ TEASPOON SALT
225 G/8 OZ UNSALTED BUTTER, AT
    ROOM TEMPERATURE
200 G/7 OZ CASTER SUGAR
2 LARGE EGGS
1 TEASPOON VANILLA ESSENCE
125 G/4 OZ WALNUTS, CHOPPED
    INTO APPROXIMATELY 5 MM/
    ¼ INCH PIECES
125 G/4 OZ PLAIN CHOCOLATE
    DROPS

Serves 12–16

Preheat the oven to 180°C/350°F/
Gas Mark 4. Butter a 33 x 22 cm/
13 x 9 inch baking tin, 5 cm/2
inches deep.

Place the dates, boiling water
and bicarbonate of soda in a food
processor and process for about
5–10 seconds or until fairly smooth
and thick.

Sift the flour, cocoa powder and
salt together.

Using an electric mixer, cream
the butter until very light, then add
the sugar, 1 tablespoon at a time,
beating until pale and fluffy. Add
the eggs, one at a time, beating
well after each addition, then beat
in the vanilla essence.

Fold in the flour mixture
alternately with the puréed dates,
beginning and ending with flour.
Spoon the mixture into the
prepared tin and spread evenly.
Sprinkle the walnuts and chocolate
drops over the top.

Bake for 40–45 minutes or
until a small skewer inserted into
the centre comes out clean. Leave
the cake to cool in the tin. Serve
cut into squares.

CINNAMON ANGEL CAKE
with almond crust

70 G/2½ OZ PLAIN FLOUR

1½ TEASPOONS GROUND
   CINNAMON

¼ TEASPOON BAKING POWDER

200 G/7 OZ CASTER SUGAR

8 LARGE EGG WHITES, AT ROOM
   TEMPERATURE

1 TEASPOON CREAM OF TARTAR

¼ TEASPOON SALT

1 TEASPOON VANILLA ESSENCE

¼ TEASPOON ALMOND ESSENCE

ALMOND CRUST

2 SMALL EGG WHITES

2½ TABLESPOONS CASTER SUGAR

125 G/4 OZ FLAKED ALMONDS
   (PREFERABLY UNBLANCHED),
   CRUMBLED

½ TEASPOON GROUND CINNAMON

SERVES 12–14

Preheat the oven to 180°C/350°F/
Gas Mark 4. Use an ungreased 22
cm/9 inch angel food (funnelled)
tin or a 22 cm/9 inch round, 8 cm/
3 inch deep cake tin. Line the base
with nonstick baking paper.

Sift the flour, cinnamon, baking
powder and 85 g/3 oz of the sugar
together four times.

Using an electric mixer, beat the
egg whites until frothy. Add the
cream of tartar, salt, vanilla and
almond essences and beat until soft
peaks form. Gradually beat in the
remaining sugar, taking 2 minutes
to incorporate it.

Sift the flour mixture over the
egg whites in five or six additions,
folding in quickly. Turn the mixture
into the tin. Circle the mixture
twice with a knife to remove air
pockets. Smooth the top.

Bake for 40–45 minutes or until
the top feels dry. Invert on to four
ramekins to support the rim of the
tin, allowing air to circulate
underneath; do not remove the tin
until the cake is cool.

Turn the tin right-side up; shake
gently to unmould the cake. Place
the cake top side up on a lightly
greased baking sheet. Preheat the
oven to 160°C/325°F/Gas Mark 3.

For the crust, whisk the egg
whites until foamy. Gradually add
1½ tablespoons of the sugar. Stir in
the almonds. Spread over the cake.
Sprinkle with the cinnamon mixed
with the remaining sugar. Bake for
20 minutes or until lightly brown.

MARBLE KUGELHOPF

40 G/1½ OZ FLAKED ALMONDS
285 G/10½ OZ PLAIN FLOUR
2 TEASPOONS BAKING POWDER
½ TEASPOON SALT
285 G/10½ OZ UNSALTED BUTTER,
    AT ROOM TEMPERATURE
¼ TEASPOON GRATED LEMON
    ZEST
¼ TEASPOON GRATED ORANGE
    ZEST
135 G/4½ OZ ICING SUGAR, SIFTED
6 LARGE EGGS, SEPARATED
2 TEASPOONS VANILLA ESSENCE
200 G/7 OZ CASTER SUGAR
2 TABLESPOONS UNSWEETENED
    COCOA POWDER
2 TABLESPOONS VEGETABLE OIL
VANILLA GLAZE (PAGE 28)

SERVES 8–10

Preheat the oven to 180°C/350°F/
Gas Mark 4. Generously butter a
24 cm/9½ inch kugelhopf tin and
sprinkle with the almonds. Sift the
flour, baking powder and salt
together three times.

Using an electric mixer, cream
the butter with the lemon and
orange zests. Add the icing sugar in
four additions, beating well. Beat in
the egg yolks, two at a time. Beat
in the vanilla essence.

In a separate bowl, beat the egg
whites until soft peaks form. Beat
in the caster sugar, 2 tablespoons at
a time, to form a soft meringue.
Fold the meringue and flour
alternately into the creamed
mixture, beginning and ending
with the meringue.

Place just over one-third of the
mixture in a separate bowl.
Combine the cocoa and oil and
fold into the mixture.

Place alternate layers of the
vanilla and chocolate mixture in
the tin, beginning and ending with
vanilla, and smooth the top.

Bake for 60–65 minutes or
until golden brown and coming
away from the sides of the tin.
Leave to cool in the tin for 15
minutes, then turn out on to a
cooling rack. Drizzle the warm
cake with vanilla glaze.

BANANA HAZELNUT TEA LOAF

200 G/7 OZ PLAIN FLOUR
1 TEASPOON BAKING POWDER
½ TEASPOON BICARBONATE OF
    SODA
½ TEASPOON SALT
100 G/3½ OZ HAZELNUTS, LIGHTLY
    TOASTED, THEN LEFT UNTIL
    COLD
2–3 SMALL RIPE BANANAS
4 TABLESPOONS ORANGE JUICE
1 TEASPOON VANILLA ESSENCE
2 LARGE EGGS
150 G/5 OZ CASTER SUGAR
125 ML/4 FL OZ SUNFLOWER OIL
VANILLA GLAZE (PAGE 28)

SERVES 8–10
Preheat the oven to 180°C/350°F/
Gas Mark 4. Generously butter a 22
x 12 x 8 cm/9 x 5 x 3 inch loaf tin
and line the base with nonstick
baking paper.

Place the flour, baking powder,
bicarbonate of soda, salt and
hazelnuts in the bowl of a food
processor. Process for 15–20
seconds or until the nuts are
chopped into small pieces. Turn
the flour and hazelnut mixture into
a bowl.

Purée the bananas in the food
processor, then measure the puree;
you need 150 ml/5 fl oz. Stir in
the orange juice and vanilla.

Using an electric mixer on
medium-high speed, beat the eggs
until foamy. Add the sugar, 1
tablespoon at a time. Still beating,
slowly pour in the oil. Fold in the
dry ingredients alternately with the
banana mixture, beginning and
ending with flour. Spoon the
mixture into the loaf tin.

Bake for 50–55 minutes or
until a small skewer inserted into
the centre comes out clean. Leave
the cake in the tin for 15 minutes,
then turn out and remove the
baking paper. Drizzle the warm
cake with vanilla glaze.

GOLDEN APPLE CHEESECAKE

2 TABLESPOONS UNSALTED BUTTER

1.1 KG/2½ LB GOLDEN DELICIOUS
APPLES, PEELED, CORED AND
THINLY SLICED

2 TEASPOONS LEMON JUICE

275 G/10 OZ CASTER SUGAR

3 TABLESPOONS CALVADOS

675 G/1½ LB CREAM CHEESE, AT
ROOM TEMPERATURE

2 TEASPOONS GRATED LEMON ZEST

1 TEASPOON VANILLA ESSENCE

250 ML/8 FL OZ SOUR CREAM

4 LARGE EGGS

2–3 TABLESPOONS APRICOT JAM,
HEATED GENTLY WITH A LITTLE
WATER, THEN RUBBED THROUGH
A FINE SIEVE

CRUST

125 G/4 OZ GINGERNUT BISCUITS,
FINELY GROUND

50 G/2 OZ FLAKED ALMONDS,
LIGHTLY TOASTED

2 TABLESPOONS SUGAR

85 G/3 OZ UNSALTED BUTTER,
MELTED AND COOLED

SERVES 10–12

For the crust, generously butter a
22 cm/9 inch springform tin. Place
the gingernut crumbs, almonds and
sugar in a food processor and chop
finely. Blend in the melted butter.
Press the crumbs on to the sides
and base of the tin. Chill.

For the cake, melt the butter in
a large frying pan. Add the apples,
lemon juice and 125 g/4 oz of the
sugar. Sauté the apples until tender.
Add the Calvados and sauté for 1
minute. Leave to cool. Spread half
of the apples over the crust.

Preheat the oven to 180°C/
350°F/Gas Mark 4. Press a double
thickness of foil around the bottom
of the springform tin.

Using an electric mixer at low
speed, combine the cream cheese,
remaining sugar, lemon zest and
vanilla. Add the sour cream, then
the eggs, one at a time. Mix until
smooth, then pour into the tin.

Bake for 55–60 minutes or until
the centre is set. Leave on a rack to
cool for 10 minutes. Spread the
remaining apples on top and glaze
with the warm apricot jam. Leave
to cool completely before serving.

FUDGE-NUT CANDY CAKE

125 G/4 OZ GOOD-QUALITY PLAIN
CHOCOLATE, FINELY CHOPPED
375 ML/12 FL OZ MILK
1 TABLESPOON INSTANT ESPRESSO
COFFEE POWDER, DISSOLVED IN
1 TEASPOON BOILING WATER
275 G/10 OZ PLAIN FLOUR
2 TEASPOONS BAKING POWDER
½ TEASPOON BICARBONATE OF
SODA
½ TEASPOON SALT
175 G/6 OZ UNSALTED BUTTER, AT
ROOM TEMPERATURE
425 G/15 OZ CASTER SUGAR
3 LARGE EGGS
1 TEASPOON VANILLA ESSENCE
FUDGE-NUT CANDY ICING
(PAGE 30)

SERVES 12–14

Preheat the oven to 180°C/350°F/
Gas Mark 4. Butter two 22 cm/9
inch round cake tins and line the
bases with nonstick baking paper.

In a saucepan over low heat,
melt the chocolate in half of the
milk, stirring until smooth. Cool to
tepid. Add the dissolved coffee to
the remaining milk. Sift the flour,
baking powder, bicarbonate of soda
and salt together three times.

Using an electric mixer, cream
the butter until very light.
Gradually add the sugar, taking 6–8
minutes to incorporate it. Add the
eggs, one at a time, beating well,
then add the chocolate mixture
and the vanilla essence.

Fold in the flour mixture
alternately with the coffee-
flavoured milk, beginning and
ending with flour. Divide the
mixture between the two tins.

Bake for 35–40 minutes or
until firm to the touch and coming
away from the sides of the tins.
Leave the tins on a cooling rack for
15 minutes, then turn out, remove
the baking paper and leave to cool
completely before filling and icing.

LEMON SPIRAL
with cream filling

5 LARGE EGGS, SEPARATED

150 G/5 OZ CASTER SUGAR

2 TABLESPOONS LEMON JUICE

1½ TEASPOONS GRATED LEMON
    ZEST

70 G/2½ OZ PLAIN FLOUR, SIFTED

½ TEASPOON CREAM OF TARTAR

⅛ TEASPOON SALT

3 TABLESPOONS ICING SUGAR, PLUS
    EXTRA FOR DUSTING

FILLING

150 G/5 OZ CASTER SUGAR

25 G/1 OZ PLAIN FLOUR

4 TABLESPOONS LEMON JUICE

1 EGG, LIGHTLY BEATEN

1 TABLESPOON GRATED LEMON
    ZEST

300 ML/½ PINT DOUBLE CREAM,
    WHIPPED UNTIL THICK

SERVES 10–12

Preheat the oven to 180°C/350°F/
Gas Mark 4. Butter the base of a
43 x 28 cm/17 x 11 inch baking
tin, 2.5 cm/1 inch deep. Line with
nonstick baking paper.

Using an electric mixer on
medium speed, beat the egg yolks
until very pale. Gradually add the
caster sugar, beat until thick, then
add the lemon juice and zest. Fold
in the flour.

In a separate bowl, beat the egg
whites until frothy. Add the cream
of tartar and beat until firm peaks
form. Fold a quarter of the whites
into the cake mixture, then gently
fold in the remaining whites. Pour
into the prepared tin.

Bake for 15 minutes or until
golden brown. Release the edges
with a knife. Invert on to a large
sheet of nonstick baking paper
dusted with the icing sugar. Peel
off the lining paper and roll up the
warm cake in the fresh paper.
Leave to cool on a cooling rack,
seam side down.

For the filling, combine all the
ingredients, except the cream, in a
bowl. Place over a saucepan of
simmering water and cook, stirring
occasionally, for 15 minutes or
until thick. Cool. Fold in the
whipped cream in three additions.
Unroll the cake, spread with two-
thirds of the lemon cream and re-
roll. To serve, decorate with the
remaining lemon cream and dust
with icing sugar.

SNOWFLAKE LAYER CAKE

325 G/12 OZ PLAIN FLOUR

4 TEASPOONS BAKING POWDER

½ TEASPOON SALT

175 ML/6 FL OZ MILK

125 ML/4 FL OZ WATER

225 G/8 OZ UNSALTED BUTTER, AT
ROOM TEMPERATURE

325 G/12 OZ CASTER SUGAR

1 LARGE EGG

1½ TEASPOONS VANILLA ESSENCE

1 TEASPOON COCONUT ESSENCE

5 LARGE EGG WHITES

½ TEASPOON CREAM OF TARTAR

VELVET BUTTERCREAM (PAGE 29)

200 G/7 OZ DESICCATED COCONUT

SERVES 12–14

Preheat the oven to 180°C/350°F/
Gas Mark 4. Butter two 22 cm/
9 inch round, 5 cm/2 inch deep
cake tins and line the bases with
nonstick baking paper. Sift the
flour, baking power and salt
together three times. Mix the milk
with the water.

Using an electric mixer on
medium speed, cream the butter
until very light. Gradually add
225 g/8 oz of the sugar, taking 6–8
minutes to incorporate it. Beat in
the egg, then the vanilla and
coconut essences.

Fold in the flour mixture
alternately with the milk and water,
beginning and ending with flour.

Whisk the egg whites until
frothy. Add the cream of tartar and
beat until soft peaks form. Add the
remaining sugar, 1 tablespoon at a
time, beating to form a soft
meringue. Fold into the cake
mixture and divide the mixture
between the prepared tins.

Bake for 30–35 minutes or until
golden brown and coming away
from the sides of the tins. Leave in
the tins on a cooling rack for 15
minutes, then turn out and remove
the baking paper.

Leave to cool completely, then
fill and coat with velvet
buttercream and cover with the
desiccated coconut.

CHOCOLATE RASPBERRY TORTE

85 G/3 OZ PLAIN FLOUR

3 TABLESPOONS UNSWEETENED
   COCOA POWDER

3 TABLESPOONS CORNFLOUR

5 LARGE EGGS

200 G/7 OZ CASTER SUGAR

1 TEASPOON VANILLA ESSENCE

3 TABLESPOONS VEGETABLE OIL

300 ML/10 FL OZ WATER

2 TABLESPOONS CREME DE
   FRAMBOISE (RASPBERRY
   LIQUEUR)

RASPBERRY VELVET
   BUTTERCREAM (PAGE 29)

CHOCOLATE SHAVINGS (PAGE 30)

FRESH RASPBERRIES (OPTIONAL)

SERVES 12–14

Preheat the oven to 180°C/350°F/
Gas Mark 4. Generously butter a
25 cm/10 inch round, 5 cm/2 inch
deep cake tin and dust with flour.
Shake out any excess flour.

Sift the flour, cocoa and
cornflour together three times.

In a mixer bowl, mix the eggs
with 150 g/5 oz of the sugar. Heat
over a saucepan of gently
simmering water, then remove
from the heat and beat with an
electric mixer on high speed for
5 minutes or until thick. Reduce
the speed to medium, add the
vanilla essence and beat for a
further 3 minutes.

Sift the flour mixture over the
egg foam in six additions, folding
in lightly with a large spatula.

Transfer a quarter of the
mixture to a separate bowl. Drizzle
in the oil while folding quickly.
Fold the two mixtures together
and pour into the prepared tin.

Bake for 30–35 minutes or
until coming away from the sides
of the tin. Invert on to a rack,
remove the tin and leave to cool.

In a small saucepan, bring the
water and remaining sugar to the
boil; simmer briefly. Remove from
the heat and add the liqueur.

Split the cake into three layers.
Place the bottom layer on a
cardboard circle. Brush generously
with warm syrup, then spread with
the raspberry buttercream. Repeat
the layering twice, then coat the
sides and top of the cake with the
remaining buttercream. Decorate
with chocolate shavings and fresh
raspberries, if available.

THE BASICS

BAKING TIPS

Successful cakes depend on the amount of air captured in the mixture, both in the creamed butter and sugar mixture, which should be beaten until very pale, light and fluffy, and in the eggs. When whisking egg whites, always use a perfectly clean, dry bowl; any trace of grease will prevent the whites from whisking to their maximum volume.

To ensure that flour is well blended with the raising agents, sift together three times; this will also aerate the mixture. The dry ingredients must be folded in evenly, but very lightly, using a large spatula or metal spoon.

Eggs and other refrigerated ingredients should be left to stand at room temperature for 20 minutes before using.

The oven rack should be positioned just below the centre of the oven.

A cake is done when firm to the touch, golden brown on top and beginning to come away from the sides of the tin. A cocktail stick or small skewer inserted into the centre should come out dry.

When icing a cake, coat the sides of the cake with a thin layer of icing, then ice the top. Finish with a second layer on the sides. Before filling and icing layer cakes, place the bottom layer top-side down and the top layer top-side up. Store iced cakes covered with aluminium foil to prevent condensation.

VANILLA GLAZE *For a 24 cm / 9½ inch cake*

In a small bowl, beat 85 g/3 oz sifted icing sugar with 1 tablespoon boiling water and ¼ teaspoon vanilla essence until smooth. Drizzle over the cake while still warm.

VELVET BUTTERCREAM

25 G/1 OZ CORNFLOUR
225 G/8 OZ CASTER SUGAR
375 ML/12 FL OZ HOT MILK
325 G/12 OZ UNSALTED BUTTER,
    AT ROOM TEMPERATURE
1½ TEASPOONS VANILLA ESSENCE
2 TABLESPOONS GRAND MARNIER
    OR COINTREAU

For a 22 cm/9 inch layer cake

In a saucepan, blend the cornflour with 85 g/3 oz of the sugar and 2 tablespoons of the hot milk. Mix until smooth. Stir in the remaining milk. Bring to the boil over low heat, stirring constantly with a whisk. Cook for 1 minute. Pour through a fine sieve and leave to cool to tepid.

Using an electric mixer, cream the butter for 1 minute. Add the remaining sugar, 1 tablespoon at a time, and beat until the mixture lightens in colour. Reduce the speed and add the tepid sauce, 1 tablespoon at a time. Mix in the vanilla and Grand Marnier.

RASPBERRY VELVET BUTTERCREAM

325 G/12 OZ FROZEN
    RASPBERRIES, PARTIALLY THAWED
85 G/3 OZ SUGAR
VELVET BUTTERCREAM (OMIT
    GRAND MARNIER)
2 TABLESPOONS CREME DE
    FRAMBOISE (RASPBERRY
    LIQUEUR)

For a 22 cm/9 inch layer cake

Place the raspberries and sugar in a saucepan. Bring to the boil and cook, uncovered, until very thick, about 12–15 minutes. Press the raspberries through a fine sieve to remove the seeds. Leave to cool before using.

Using an electric mixer on low speed, add the raspberry purée to the buttercream. Flavour with the raspberry liqueur.

FUDGE-NUT CANDY ICING

125 G/4 OZ + 2 TABLESPOONS
   UNSALTED BUTTER
175 G/6 OZ GOOD-QUALITY PLAIN
   CHOCOLATE, CHOPPED
175 G/6 OZ DARK BROWN SUGAR
2 TABLESPOONS LIGHT CORN SYRUP
   (LIQUID GLUCOSE)
¼ TEASPOON SALT
2 TEASPOONS INSTANT ESPRESSO
   COFFEE POWDER
125 ML/4 FL OZ BOILING WATER
300 G/11 OZ ICING SUGAR, SIFTED
1½ TEASPOONS VANILLA ESSENCE
1 TEASPOON LEMON JUICE
125 G/4 OZ TOASTED WALNUTS,
   ROUGHLY CHOPPED

For a 22 cm/9 inch layer cake

Place 125 g/4 oz butter, the chocolate, brown sugar, corn syrup (liquid glucose) and salt in a large saucepan. Dissolve the coffee powder in the water and add to the saucepan. Slowly bring to the boil, then simmer for 3 minutes, stirring occasionally.

Remove from the heat and whisk in the icing sugar in three additions. Stir in the vanilla and lemon juice. Add the remaining butter and beat until smooth and shiny. Stir in the walnuts. Set the pan in a bowl of ice-cold water; stir until thickened, but still warm. If the icing becomes too stiff to spread, reheat.

CHOCOLATE SHAVINGS

Place a 50 g/2 oz block of good-quality plain chocolate in a bowl in a microwave oven. Microwave for 10 seconds on defrost.

Turn the chocolate over and microwave for a further 10 seconds. Put the chocolate on a cutting board. Using a sharp 20 cm/8 inch knife, cut the chocolate into thin shavings.

THE MASTER CHEFS

SOUPS
ARABELLA BOXER

MEZE, TAPAS AND ANTIPASTI
AGLAIA KREMEZI

PASTA SAUCES
GORDON RAMSAY

RISOTTO
MICHELE SCICOLONE

SALADS
CLARE CONNERY

MEDITERRANEAN
ANTONY WORRALL THOMPSON

VEGETABLES
PAUL GAYLER

LUNCHES
ALASTAIR LITTLE

COOKING FOR TWO
RICHARD OLNEY

FISH
RICK STEIN

CHICKEN
BRUNO LOUBET

SUPPERS
VALENTINA HARRIS

THE MAIN COURSE
ROGER VERGÉ

ROASTS
JANEEN SARLIN

WILD FOOD
ROWLEY LEIGH

PACIFIC
JILL DUPLEIX

CURRIES
PAT CHAPMAN

HOT AND SPICY
PAUL AND JEANNE RANKIN

THAI
JACKI PASSMORE

CHINESE
YAN-KIT SO

VEGETARIAN
KAREN LEE

DESSERTS
MICHEL ROUX

CAKES
CAROLE WALTER

COOKIES
ELINOR KLIVANS

THE MASTER CHEFS

This edition produced for The Book People Ltd,

Hall Wood Avenue, Haydock, St Helens WAII 9UL

Text © copyright 1996 Carole Walter

Carole Walter has asserted her right to be
identified as the Author of this Work.

Photographs © copyright 1996 Simon Wheeler

First published in 1996 by

WEIDENFELD & NICOLSON

THE ORION PUBLISHING GROUP

ORION HOUSE

5 UPPER ST MARTIN'S LANE

LONDON WC2H 9EA

British Library Cataloguing-in-Publication data
A catalogue record for this book is available
from the British Library.

ISBN 0 297 83647 1

DESIGNED BY THE SENATE

EDITOR MAGGIE RAMSAY

FOOD STYLIST JOY DAVIES

ASSISTANT KATY HOLDER